CW01512894

Original title:
Mottled Branches Along the Wizard Chain

Author: Daisy Dewi
ISBN HARDBACK: 978-1-80559-242-6
ISBN PAPERBACK: 978-1-80559-741-4

Threads of Fable in the Wildwood

In the wildwood, whispers play,
Sunlight dances, drifting ray.
Old trees shelter tales untold,
Life's secrets wrapped in green and gold.

A brook babbles songs of yore,
Winding paths through nature's door.
Each step soft, upon the ground,
Echoes of the lost can be found.

Mossy stones, they softly gleam,
As shadows weave a timeless dream.
The wind's embrace, a gentle sigh,
Cradles the stories passing by.

Moonlit nights, the stars ignite,
In the forest, magic's sprite.
Hushed voices call from afar,
Guiding hearts where wonders are.

With each thread of fable spun,
Life unfolds, a tale begun.
In the wildwood, lost yet found,
A tapestry of life unbound.

Kaleidoscope of the Ancient Arbor

Leaves whisper tales of old,
Colors dance in vibrant gold.
Roots that twist in dark embrace,
A tapestry of time and space.

Branches cradle dreams undone,
Sunlight filters, soft and fun.
Nature's canvas, bold and bright,
In the shadows, secrets light.

Secrets Weaved in Twilight Canopy

Beneath the veil of dusk's soft sigh,
Stories linger, low and shy.
Mossy carpets hide the truth,
Among the echoes of lost youth.

Fingers stroke the silken night,
Stars become the dreams in flight.
Crickets sing the ancient song,
In the dark, where hearts belong.

Threads of the Sorcerer's Boughs

Magic weaves through every branch,
Whispers beckon, shadows dance.
Gnarled limbs reach towards the skies,
A world awakens, where magic lies.

Beneath the bark, stories sleep,
In twilight's grasp, their secrets keep.
Moonlit paths through myths are drawn,
The sorcerer's touch at every dawn.

Echoes from the Twisted Limbs

A rustle speaks of ancient lore,
Twisted limbs, they want to soar.
In the breeze, a haunting song,
Echoes of the past belong.

Sunbeams pierce the thicket tight,
Revealing shadows drenched in light.
Beneath the boughs, a story stirs,
In silence, nature softly purrs.

The Enigma of Twisted Ferns

In shadows deep, the ferns entwine,
Their spirals dance, a mystery divine.
Rooted secrets, nature's guise,
Whispers soft, beneath the skies.

With emerald trails, they curl and sway,
An ancient code in green array.
Each twist and turn, a tale unfolds,
Of timeless dreams, and earth's strong holds.

Beneath the canopy, silence reigns,
Where sunlight filters, softly it wanes.
Endless stories in each frond's embrace,
The enigma lives—a sacred space.

Whispers Beneath the Gnarled Crown

Beneath the crown where shadows play,
Gnarled branches weave the light of day.
Secrets murmur in the breeze,
Echoing through the ancient trees.

Rustling leaves, they share their tales,
Of quiet strength and timeless trails.
Each knot and bend, a history traced,
In the bark's embrace, ages are faced.

Moonlit nights bring haunting dreams,
As silver beams cast gentle gleams.
The whispers grow in the stillness of night,
Beneath the crown, hearts take flight.

Ethereal Vines of Bejeweled Shade

In twilight's glow, the vines entwine,
With jeweled leaves, they softly shine.
A tapestry of colors bold,
In secret havens, stories told.

The gentle sway of bejeweled grace,
In nature's arms, we find our place.
Each tendril wraps with tender care,
A tranquil dance, a lover's snare.

Hidden paths, where shadows play,
Ethereal whispers guide the way.
Through vibrant hues and fragrant air,
In jeweled shade, we find despair.

Dreamweaver's Path Among the Foliage

Amidst the green, the dreamers tread,
On paths where sunlight fears to spread.
The foliage whispers secrets deep,
In woven dreams, we laugh and weep.

Each step reveals a hidden door,
To realms of wonder, and so much more.
The wild refrain of nature calls,
In tangled beauty, hope enthralls.

With gentle hands, the dreamweaver guides,
Through lush embrace where magic hides.
In every leaf, a promise gleams,
A journey forged of wildest dreams.

Riddles Woven in Knotted Wood

In the forest where secrets twine,
Ancient trees with tales enshrined.
Knots and whorls like puzzles laid,
Whispering truths that time has played.

Shadows dance in dappled light,
Riddles lurking, out of sight.
Roots entwined in earthen lore,
Holding mysteries evermore.

A glint of hope in bark so old,
Stories of life quietly told.
Voices echo in winds that sigh,
As the spirits of timber lie.

Branches stretch to embrace the sky,
Yearning for dreams that never die.
Life, death, in silence blend,
Nature's riddle, without end.

In the heart of a knotted glade,
A labyrinth where whispers fade.
Timbers guard the tales they've spun,
In their embrace, we are all one.

The Arcane Dance of Bark and Canopy

Under the veil of twilight's glow,
Canopies swirl, a silent show.
Bark adorned with runes of old,
An arcane dance, a tale retold.

Leaves shimmer with a spectral light,
In their folds, the shadows fight.
Branches twine in a mystic braid,
Nature's pulse, a serenade.

The forest breathes with ancient sighs,
Unraveling truth in the skies.
Echoes of laughter cling to air,
A symphony wrought with tender care.

Twisting forms in the moonlit beam,
Nature's magic flows like a dream.
Companions of splendor, wild and free,
In this realm, we weave a decree.

As night falls, the dance ascends,
Eternity bound, the spiral bends.
In the cadence of bark and leaves,
The arcane tale of life believes.

Twilit Paths Through the Limber Grove

Through paths where light is softly draped,
Limber trees with shadows shaped.
Twilit whispers guide the way,
In dusk's embrace, we long to stay.

Leaves rustle with secrets untold,
Nature's breath, both warm and cold.
Beneath the boughs, our footsteps roam,
Finding solace, a place called home.

Twilight hues of deepened blue,
Brush the branches, a calming view.
Where light and dark gently entwine,
In this grove, our souls align.

The scent of earth, a fragrant veil,
In soft laughter, we find our trail.
With every step, the twilight speaks,
Of forgotten dreams and mystic peaks.

So let us wander, hearts in tow,
Through limber paths, where wild things grow.
In twilight's arms, we'll forever roam,
The beauty of nature, our cherished home.

Echoes of the Eldritch Thicket

In the thicket where shadows hide,
Echoes linger, far and wide.
Bramble whispers, secrets spun,
Guard the tales of old and done.

With every rustle, ancient sighs,
Unravel truths beneath the skies.
Mysteries cloaked in shades of green,
Haunting visions, seldom seen.

Twisted branches weave a spell,
In the depths of this verdant well.
Each thorn and leaf, a whispered word,
In the silence, voices stirred.

The heart of the thicket beats so strong,
A primal rhythm, a timeless song.
In this realm where spirits loom,
Shadows gather, embracing gloom.

Yet amidst the dark, a flicker glows,
Illuminating what each heart knows.
In echoes found within the thorn,
The eldritch thicket is reborn.

Harmonies in the Hollow Canopy

Leaves whisper secrets, soft and low,
Sunlight dances on the forest's glow.
Birds sing melodies, rich and sweet,
Nature's choir, where shadows meet.

Roots embrace earth, deep and wide,
Branches sway with the wind's gentle tide.
Time weaves stories through the trees,
In this sanctuary, hearts find ease.

Moss carpets paths where travelers roam,
Each step taken, a story grown.
Breezes carry a fragrant tune,
Under the watch of the silver moon.

Echoes of laughter dance through the night,
Glowing fireflies sprinkle delight.
Together in harmony, we sway,
Lost in the beauty, we choose to stay.

Nature's embrace, a comforting sight,
In the hollow canopy, purest light.
Here, we find solace and peace anew,
In the whispers of leaves and morning dew.

The Spellbound Journey of Twined Vines

Twined vines spiral in a mystic kiss,
Nature's embrace, a world of bliss.
Every twist tells a tale of old,
Secrets of forests in green and gold.

They wander through shadows, weaving tight,
Binding the earth with threads of light.
Under the canopy, dreams take flight,
In a spellbound journey, pure delight.

Around ancient trunks, they charmingly dance,
A swirling ballet, a graceful chance.
Life intertwines, as moments unfold,
In the tapestry woven, vibrant and bold.

With each turn, the stories unwind,
Of fairies and sprites, a magic entwined.
Amidst the silence, a soft refrain,
Inviting all wanderers to remain.

The path is a whisper, soft as a sigh,
Guided by starlight that paints the sky.
In this enchanted embrace we find,
A journey eternal, forever entwined.

Reverie Among the Mystic Roots

In the heart of the woods, where dreams do lay,
Mystic roots whisper, guiding the way.
Beneath the surface, secrets reside,
In the stillness of earth, where spirits abide.

With fingers tracing the ancient paths,
Each twist and gnarled branch a story that lasts.
Lost in reverie, we journey deep,
Where time slows down, inviting us to keep.

Sunlight filters through the leafy dome,
A sanctuary found, a sacred home.
Among the roots, our thoughts take flight,
Unraveling dreams in the soft twilight.

Echoes of laughter linger in the air,
A dance of memories woven with care.
Here in the stillness, we shed our fears,
Embraced by the woods, washed clean of tears.

As shadows lengthen and twilight calls,
We honor the silence as the evening falls.
In this sacred grove, together we stand,
Lost in reverie, hand in hand.

Imprints of Arcane Spirits in the Wood

In the twilight mist, spirits reside,
Echoes of magic all around abide.
Soft whispers weave through the ancient trees,
Imprints of tales carried by the breeze.

Footsteps of fairies dance on the ground,
In shadowy corners, enchantment found.
The air is tinged with stories untold,
As night unfolds its blanket of gold.

Glimmers of starlight awaken the night,
Illuminating paths with a silvery light.
We trace the lines where energies flow,
Guided by spirits that ebb and glow.

Branches entwine, sheltering dreams,
In this woodland haven where mystique gleams.
We listen closely as time holds its breath,
Embracing the whispers of life and of death.

The sacred breath of the forest we feel,
Binding our hearts to the ancient deal.
As arcane spirits beckon us near,
In the wood's embrace, we conquer our fear.

Enigmas in the Dappled Refuge

Sunlight weaves through leaves,
Shadows dance on the ground.
Whispers of secrets float,
Nature's tales all around.

Moss blankets the old stones,
Time's hand gently caresses.
Roots intertwine with stories,
Life's thread never confesses.

Birds serenade the morning,
Echoes fill the soft air.
Each twig tells a secret,
A puzzle hidden there.

Hidden gems in the thicket,
A stream sings with delight.
Every glance bears an answer,
In the hush of twilight.

Boundless paths filled with wonder,
Where dreams and truth entwine.
In this refuge of dapple,
The heart and soul align.

The Spellbound Veins of Ancient Trees

Bark worn thick with history,
Branches stretch toward the sky.
In their shade, dreams linger,
As the world rushes by.

Veins of life run deep within,
Whispering of days gone by.
Silent witnesses to time,
With a wisdom none deny.

Leaves murmur in the wind,
Secrets carried on the breeze.
Each rustle spins a story,
Of the earth beneath the trees.

Roots embrace the ancient ground,
Holding fast to myths untold.
In their grasp, the echoes play,
Memories of the bold.

Nature's timeless magic here,
In the arms of sturdy boughs.
Through each ring, the past unfolds,
In the silent vows.

Curves of Mystery in the Green Realm

Winding paths through the trees,
Twists that beckon and tease.
With each curve, a new sight,
Nature's wonders, pure and bright.

Ferns unfurl like secrets,
In the quiet, shadows hide.
The dance of light and dark,
In this realm where dreams reside.

Hushed whispers of the forest,
Songbirds call from afar.
Every turn holds a promise,
A new gift beneath the stars.

Colors blend in harmony,
Brushstrokes of vibrant glee.
Each curve tells a story,
In this realm of mystery.

Through the deep and the light,
The heart sways with delight.
In this dance of the wild,
Find solace in the night.

The Enchanted Intertwine of Nature

Vines wrap around the trees,
Embracing with gentle grace.
In their touch, a bond forms,
A dance time cannot erase.

Petals drift on the wind,
Carried far from their home.
Every flower tells a tale,
In this interwoven dome.

Water glistens like jewels,
Reflecting a world anew.
In its flow, we see echoes,
Of a sky, a vast blue.

Mountains stand as watchers,
Guardians of stories old.
Nature's heart beats steady,
In their embrace, so bold.

In this realm intertwined,
Find the magic that thrives.
Within nature's endless weave,
The truest joy arrives.

Whispers of Enchanted Twigs

In twilight's grasp, the whispers call,
Soft secrets shared, a gentle thrall.
Among the twigs, the voices weave,
A tapestry of dreams to believe.

The sighing leaves, they dance and sway,
Beneath a sky that fades to gray.
Each rustling breeze brings tales of old,
Of magic held and hearts consoled.

With every step on mossy ground,
The rhythms of the earth resound.
In shadows deep, the spirits dwell,
Their stories spun, where echoes swell.

The moon unveils a silver thread,
Leading the lost where few have tread.
Through tangled roots and hopeful sighs,
The whispers rise, beneath the skies.

So linger long, in twilight's hue,
Let whispers soft, embrace you too.
For in the dark, where wonders gleam,
The enchanted twigs will craft your dream.

Shadows of the Mystic Grove

In shadows deep, where silence breathes,
The ancient trees sway, their secrets sheathe.
A mystic grove, untouched by time,
Holds stories lost, in rhythmic rhyme.

Beneath the boughs, a chill does creep,
As twilight weaves its spell, so deep.
Whispers linger, a ghostly tune,
A serenade by the watchful moon.

Moss cloaks the ground in velvet green,
Where light and dark begin to glean.
Each rustle carries a soft lament,
A bridge to realms where the lost are sent.

Through brambles thick, the legends flow,
In shadows cast, the spirits know.
Each step reveals a truth concealed,
A world of wonders, softly revealed.

So wander here, in twilight's thrall,
Where shadows dance and nightbirds call.
Embrace the mystery, quiet and stark,
For in this grove, the magic spark.

Hues of the Forest Enchantment

In morning light, where colors bloom,
Hues of enchantment dispel the gloom.
Emerald leaves in glistening rays,
Drape the forest in a vibrant haze.

Crimson petals on the forest floor,
Whisper tales of what came before.
Golden sunlight through branches breaks,
Painting shadows, as daylight wakes.

A canvas brushed by nature's hand,
Each hue a thread in this vibrant land.
With every step, the story unfolds,
A symphony of colors, bolds and golds.

From misty morn to evening's sigh,
The forest shifts beneath the sky.
In hues so bright, and shades so rare,
Magic blossoms in the crisp, cool air.

So breathe it in, this tranquil grace,
As colors blend and hearts embrace.
In the forest's hues, both rich and bright,
You'll find the spark that ignites the night.

Veins of the Eldritch Silhouette

In twilight's shadow, darkness sprawls,
The silhouette of magic calls.
Veins of wonder in the air,
Pulse with secrets, old and rare.

Branches twist, like fingers curled,
Guarding mysteries of the world.
Beneath the stars, where shadows blend,
The eldritch whispers never end.

The starlit path, a winding thread,
Guides the way where few have tread.
Echoes dance on the cool night air,
A symphony of dusk laid bare.

In ancient groves, where creatures roam,
The veins of night feel just like home.
With every gaze upon the sky,
The eldritch calls, a haunting sigh.

So delve into the shadows near,
Embrace the magic, void of fear.
For in the dark, where wonders meet,
The eldritch veins shall guide your feet.

Fables Hidden in the Leafy Labyrinth

In twisted paths where shadows play,
Whispers of the past find their way.
Ancient tales in green embrace,
Lost in time, yet full of grace.

Each turn conceals a story old,
Where secrets tread, the brave behold.
A winding road of heart and mind,
With echoes of the truth entwined.

Beneath the boughs a chorus sings,
Of creatures born from ancient things.
Their voices weave through branches wide,
A fable cherished, never died.

The sunlight dapples on the ground,
In every crevice, wonder found.
A map of dreams within the leaves,
In every rustle, magic weaves.

So wander deep, let senses lead,
Through labyrinths where spirits feed.
For fables whisper soft and low,
In leafy halls where secrets grow.

Glimmers Through the Verdant Veil

In morning's light, a soft embrace,
The verdant veil reveals its grace.
With every step, the world anew,
A canvas painted in every hue.

Through emerald leaves, the sun does peek,
Like hidden gems, so bright, unique.
Each ray that dances on the ground,
Holds tales untold, waiting to be found.

The whispers of the gentle breeze,
Carry hints of forgotten trees.
Where shadows play and soft winds sigh,
A symphony beneath the sky.

Glimmers spark in every nook,
As heart and nature intertwine their look.
In silence, secrets softly kept,
In leafy realms where dreams have crept.

So wander forth, let wonder steer,
Through hidden paths, both bright and clear.
For in the veil's embrace you'll find,
The magic that the heart entwined.

Mythic Canopy of the Celestial Wood

Above, the stars in silence glow,
Underneath, the earth below.
A mythic world where spirits dwell,
In every branch, a tale to tell.

The canopy, a vast expanse,
Where shadows swirl in twilight dance.
A realm where dreams and stories blend,
In every twist, beginnings, end.

Twinkling lights like thoughts take flight,
In the hush of softest night.
The ancient trees hold wisdom still,
A testament to nature's will.

As whispers float on gentle air,
The heart can truly learn to care.
For in this wood, the myths arise,
A tapestry beneath the skies.

So seek the paths within the green,
Where myth and magic can be seen.
And in the quiet, let it be,
A journey deep to set you free.

Secrets of the Twilight Thicket

As dusk descends, the shadows creep,
In twilight thickets, secrets keep.
The world transforms in golden haze,
Where whispers echo through the maze.

Beneath the boughs, a rustle sounds,
An invitation in the rounds.
With every footfall, stories weave,
In twilight's grip, it's hard to leave.

The air is thick with tales untold,
Of ancient beasts and treasures bold.
A magic lingers, soft and sweet,
In every corner, life's heartbeat.

So lay your worries, take a breath,
In nature's arms, there's life, not death.
Explore the paths where shadows blend,
To find the wisdom that they send.

In twilight thickets, secrets spin,
In every echo, the world begins.
With heart wide open, journey deep,
To unearth treasures the woods do keep.

Whispers of Twisted Shadows

In the night where whispers creep,
Shadows dance, secrets to keep.
Twisted limbs, a silent song,
Echoes of where they belong.

Moonlight glimmers, soft and pale,
Casting paths where dreams set sail.
Nature's breath in twilight's cloak,
Voices stir, and spirits evoke.

Beneath the stars, a mystery grows,
In the depths of tangled throes.
Each sigh a tale, each breath a plea,
Woven tight with destiny.

Flickering lights in the silent trees,
A gentle hum sways with the breeze.
In the hush, old murmurs sigh,
Twisted shadows, lullabies nigh.

Fading thoughts where the dark hides,
Awakening echoes, the heart confides.
Listen close; they softly call,
Whispers trapped within the thrall.

An Enchantment of Weathered Boughs

Ancient trees with boughs so wise,
Whisper tales under soft, blue skies.
Leaves that chatter in gentle winds,
Secrets spun where the forest begins.

A soft hum flows through knotted twine,
Time's embrace on each weathered line.
Evergreen thoughts, memories old,
Guarding stories waiting to be told.

Sunlight dapples, a fleeting glance,
Nature's charms in a graceful dance.
Gnarled roots twist deep in the earth,
Cradling echoes of laughter and mirth.

In the stillness, shadows sway,
Guiding footsteps on nature's way.
All who wander find comfort here,
Weathered boughs, forever near.

Each rustling leaf, a promise gleaned,
An enchantment born of all we dreamed.
In this haven, our hearts align,
Under the canopy, pure and divine.

Secrets of the Gnarled Arbor

Beneath the canopy, secrets lie,
In gnarled branches reaching high.
Whispers of ages linger sweet,
Among the roots where shadows meet.

Time etched deep in each twisted vein,
Stories held in wood and grain.
Softly sighing with every gust,
A sacred pact, a timeless trust.

Cloaked in green, a world unfolds,
The gnarled arbor holds truths untold.
From bark to leaf, a tale to spin,
Of life, of loss, where love begins.

In twilight's glow, dreams intertwine,
Cradle your heart with nature's sign.
Each fleeting moment, a spark so bright,
Gnarled branches weave in the soft twilight.

With every breath, the forest speaks,
To weary souls, to truth it seeks.
Secrets cradled in whispers' glow,
In the gnarled arbor, time moves slow.

Charmed Limbs Beneath the Crescent

Beneath the crescent, soft and bright,
Charmed limbs dance in the silver light.
Every sway, a story shared,
In fragrant blooms, our souls bared.

Glimmers of magic in the cool night air,
A symphony echoes, vibrant and rare.
Crickets serenade, the stars align,
In this embrace where hearts entwine.

Each gentle rustle, a lover's tune,
Beneath the watchful, glowing moon.
Gathered dreams on branches weave,
Charmed moments, we'll never leave.

Silhouetted whispers beckon near,
As shadows shimmer, all is clear.
In the garden where wonders bloom,
We find our solace, dispelling gloom.

With every heartbeat, nature calls,
A lullaby where magic falls.
Charmed limbs cradle our fears away,
Beneath the crescent, we'll forever stay.

Beneath the Canopy of Curious Knots

Under the branches, shadows dance,
Whispers of nature, a fleeting chance.
Twisting vines that tightly weave,
Tales of the forest, if you believe.

Mossy carpets beneath our feet,
A world alive, both strange and sweet.
Curled leaves cradle secrets old,
Stories of life in patterns bold.

Each knot tells a tale, a soft refrain,
Echoes of rain, the touch of pain.
Glimmers of sunlight break the gloom,
Beneath the canopy, endless bloom.

A symphony plays in rustling leaves,
Nature's heartbeat that never deceives.
Between the branches, dreams take flight,
In the depths, we find our light.

Here, time dances, a gentle flow,
Amongst the knots, we learn to grow.
Beneath the whispers, a sacred trove,
In the forest's heart, we find our grove.

The Sylvan Tapestry of Wonders

In every glade, a tale unfolds,
With threads of green and hints of gold.
Sunbeams filter through the trees,
Painting stories with each breeze.

Murmurs of streams in soft embrace,
Nature's brush creates its space.
Ferns unfurl like ancient scrolls,
Guarding secrets of timeless souls.

Wildflowers bloom in vibrant hues,
Nature's palette, a curious muse.
Whispers of creatures call from afar,
Guided by the light of the evening star.

In the heart of woods, magic thrives,
Where the spirit of every tree survives.
A dance of shadows, a play of light,
In the tapestry woven, the world's delight.

Beneath the boughs, we lose our fear,
In the sylvan song, all becomes clear.
Every step reveals a new glance,
In nature's embrace, we find our chance.

Secrets Spun in the Twilight Glade

When dusk descends and shadows play,
In twilight's glow, the whispers sway.
Spiders spin with diligent care,
Webs of dreams, delicate and rare.

Glimmers of hope in the fading light,
Echoes of day yield to the night.
Beneath the stars, the world holds its breath,
In the gentle shroud of impending rest.

Mossy stones guard silent lore,
Tales of the past, forevermore.
Each sigh of wind carries a sound,
The secrets of life that abound.

Crisp leaves rustle in soft delight,
Guiding the way, a fragile sight.
In the twilight glade, time slows its race,
Moments suspended, a warm embrace.

Each flicker of light ignites the dark,
Every heartbeat, a vital spark.
In the hush of night, our spirits gleam,
In shadows spun, we dare to dream.

The Hieroglyphs of Leaf and Limb

Nature writes on bark and bone,
Stories etched in every throne.
Hieroglyphs whisper in the breeze,
Each symbol tells of ancient trees.

Leaves like pages flutter and fight,
Capturing moments in the light.
Roots entwined beneath the ground,
A language of silence, profound.

Branches arch in a graceful pose,
A dance of life, as the river flows.
Every twig, a history traced,
Under the sun, where shadows embraced.

In the forest's arms, wisdom thrives,
In the quiet hum, true life survives.
Hieroglyphs speak to hearts that hear,
In nature's text, we draw near.

Awake the senses, feel the pulse,
In every rustle, nature's impulse.
Amongst the leaves, a story gleams,
In the heart of woods, we weave our dreams.

A Symphony in the Whispering Wood

Leaves hum softly in the breeze,
Sunlight flickers through the trees.
Birds compose their sweet refrain,
Nature's choir calls again.

A brook babbles, secrets shared,
Every note, a moment spared.
With each rustle, stories glide,
In the woods, where dreams reside.

Branches sway in rhythmic grace,
Creating shadows, a soft embrace.
Echoes weave through tranquil air,
A symphony, beyond compare.

Footsteps light on forest floor,
Adventures wait 'neath ancient lore.
Whispers tell of times long past,
In this realm where moments last.

A gentle hush, all hearts align,
In the woods, where souls entwine.
Nature's love, a sacred bond,
In this haven, we respond.

Shadows Danced by Fabled Wind

Moonlight drapes the quiet glade,
Whispers rise as dreams invade.
Shadows flicker, ancient lore,
Secrets linger, evermore.

Winds weave tales of ages past,
Each soft breath, a spell is cast.
Echoes whisper through the night,
Guiding footsteps, lost from sight.

Glimmers spark in midnight's hue,
Tales unfold as shadows grew.
Mysteries spin with each gust,
In the dark, we place our trust.

Dancing leaves upon the breeze,
Nature's rhythm aims to please.
Every rustle sings a tune,
Mirroring the crescent moon.

Silhouettes of branches play,
In the heat of twilight's sway.
Fabled winds call us to roam,
In this dance, we find our home.

The Labyrinth of Nature's Secrets

In the thicket, paths entwine,
Nature's secrets, pure design.
Twisting trails, shadows entwined,
Mysteries wake, knowledge blind.

Ferns rise high, in whispered cheer,
To guide us through, they reappear.
Echoed calls from distant trees,
Every turn, a chance to seize.

Twilight flickers, fading light,
Illuminates the coming night.
Steps reveal what hearts can feel,
In this maze, the truth is real.

Hidden glens hold precious words,
In their depths, lost dreams are stirred.
Labyrinths of leaf and vine,
Nature's voice, a sign divine.

Through the wild, we seek, we find,
Woven tales of heart and mind.
With each step, the world unveils,
Secrets whispered on the trails.

Enchanted Roots and Swaying Tales

Beneath the soil, roots embrace,
Whispers cradle every trace.
Tales of ages, soft and low,
In the shadows, stories grow.

Branches sway like dancers' arms,
Lulling hearts with nature's charms.
Every breeze, a spell is cast,
In their cradle, time amassed.

Petals fall like dreams in flight,
Fragrant wishes, pure delight.
Creeping vines entwining way,
Holding time in soft array.

Roots that dig into the past,
Link the future to the vast.
Whispers of the earth's own heart,
From these tales, we'll never part.

In the thicket, stories flow,
Swaying softly, like the snow.
Enchanted tales bind us all,
In their magic, we stand tall.

The Allure of Fragmented Flora

In whispers soft, the petals sway,
Colorful shards in bright display.
A tapestry of nature's art,
Each fragment plays a crucial part.

Beneath the sun, they catch the light,
Dancing gently in sheer delight.
A vivid world, so vast, so spry,
Where beauty blooms and dreams can fly.

In the quiet of a summer's day,
Their fragrance drifts, a sweet ballet.
Among the thorns, the beauty thrives,
In shifting winds, the heart derives.

With every twist, a story told,
Of life's embrace, both young and old.
The petals shimmer, pure and true,
A canvas painted, life anew.

In this world of fragmented grace,
Nature's charm finds every place.
Through fading light, they hold their ground,
In fleeting moments, beauty found.

Echoes of the Hidden Canopy

Above the world, a shelter stands,
With whispered secrets, nature's hands.
Through leaves that flutter, soft and low,
Echoes linger where shadows flow.

The canopy, a sheltered dome,
A tranquil spot, a quiet home.
Where sunlight dapples with soft embrace,
And time stands still in this lush space.

Nestled high, birds weave their songs,
Melodies sweet; they all belong.
In shadows deep, the stories rise,
A gentle world beneath the skies.

With every breeze that weaves through limbs,
Nature hums her ancient hymns.
The rustle whispers tales of old,
Of life and growth, in green enfold.

Here in the arboreal deep,
Echoes dance, while the forest sleeps.
Their murmurs blend with rustling leaves,
A symphony that heart perceives.

Secrets Murmured Among Elder Branches

In ancient woods, where shadows lie,
The elder branches reach the sky.
Their gnarled forms a tale to share,
Of whispered secrets hanging there.

With every creak, they speak of time,
Of seasons spent in silent rhyme.
Their leaves, like pages, turn and sway,
In stories told through night and day.

Beneath their boughs, the magic stirs,
A treasure trove of life concurs.
Soft murmurs pass through every bough,
And in their shade, we wonder how.

Through changing skies, the branches bend,
In quiet strength, their forms extend.
Roots deep in earth, they hold their claim,
In nature's heart, a sacred name.

Among the elder, secrets bloom,
In filtered light, dispelling gloom.
A gentle world where wisdom reigns,
And every winding path remains.

The Alluring Dance of Shadowed Leaves

In twilight's glow, the shadows play,
Leaves flutter softly, night meets day.
A dance unfolds beneath the trees,
Where tender whispers brush the breeze.

With every twist, a story's spun,
Of fleeting moments, shadows run.
They overlap in a graceful art,
Brush strokes of darkness, nature's heart.

Through branches swaying, laughter rings,
While crickets serenade with strings.
In this realm of whispered dreams,
The shadowed leaves weave mystic themes.

As moonlight drapes a silver veil,
The woodland's charm begins to sail.
In soft embrace, they twirl and glide,
An alluring dance, where dreams reside.

Caught in the night, the beauty gleams,
Nature's whispers, enchanting dreams.
In shadow's grace, the world can see,
The alluring dance of it all, free.

The Color of Forgotten Echoes

Whispers of time in shades of grey,
Memories linger, they fade away.
Silent shadows dance on the floor,
Colors of dreams behind closed door.

In the dim light, secrets unfold,
Tales of the past in whispers told.
Echoes of laughter weave through the night,
A tapestry woven in soft twilight.

Hues of emotion painted in sighs,
Mirroring moments that never die.
Fleeting glimpses, a soft caress,
The color of life in its vastness.

Faded portraits on dusty walls,
Time's gentle hand gracefully calls.
In the silence, stories arise,
Reflections concealed behind our eyes.

In every stroke, the heart reveals,
A canvas of all that it feels.
The color of echoes, forever bright,
Guiding our souls through the night.

Labyrinths of Nature's Wonder

In the forest deep, secrets lie,
Beneath the branches, the earth can sigh.
Twisting pathways, unseen ahead,
Nature's embrace where dreams are fed.

Moss-covered stones, whispers of trees,
Songs of the wind in the gentle breeze.
Colors colliding in vibrant hues,
Nature's palette, both bold and true.

Delicate petals, soft as a sigh,
Bees on a mission, buzzing nearby.
Winding paths that lead us astray,
In a maze of wonders, we long to stay.

With every step, a story unfolds,
In every crevice, nature's gold.
From rivers to mountains, beauty thrives,
In labyrinths where adventure survives.

A journey through whispers of green,
Where every moment feels like a dream.
Nature's wonder, a treasure chest,
In the heart of the wild, we find our rest.

Breath of Ancients in Gnarled Limbs

In the embrace of ancient trees,
Stories breathe with every breeze.
Gnarled limbs reaching toward the sky,
Guardians of time that never die.

Roots cradled deep in the earth's core,
Whispering sagas of those before.
Leaves rustle softly, secrets share,
The breath of ancients fills the air.

Time-worn bark tells a tale or two,
Of creatures wild and storms that blew.
Nature's wisdom in every ring,
An ode to life, the songs they sing.

In twilight's glow, shadows entwine,
The past and present, delicately align.
With every heartbeat, tales unspool,
The breath of ancients, timeless and fuel.

In quiet moments, we stand in awe,
For the stories told are never raw.
In gnarled limbs, a legacy thrives,
In each breath, the ancients' lives.

Vestiges of Unknown Enchantment

In the twilight where shadows dwell,
Echoes of magic weave a spell.
Whispers of wonder linger near,
Vestiges of dreams that disappear.

Glimmers of light in the darkened glade,
Hints of enchantment that softly fade.
Mysterious trails lead us to seek,
The secrets of silence, shy and meek.

Crimson blooms in a sea of night,
Fleeting glimpses of lost delight.
In hidden corners of forgotten lands,
Enchanted moments slip through our hands.

With every step, a new dawn breaks,
The heart remembers what our soul aches.
In silent realms, the whispers arise,
Vestiges of magic in quiet skies.

In the depths of night, the stars align,
In pursuit of mysteries, we intertwine.
For enchantment lies in each winding way,
In vestiges of dreams that never sway.

The Soul's Path Through Verdant Shadows

In the depths of green, whispers flow,
Ancient roots in twilight grow.
Each step forward, quiet and slow,
Guided softly where the heart may go.

Dappled light through leaves descends,
Secrets spoken as the forest bends.
An echo of laughter that never ends,
In this realm where the spirit mends.

A breeze carries stories untold,
Of wanderers brave and hearts bold.
A tapestry woven of threads of gold,
In the verdant shadows, mysteries unfold.

The path curves gently, winding anew,
With every turn, a different view.
In the embrace of nature's hue,
The soul finds peace, ever true.

And as the sun dips low and fades,
The journey whispers in mysterious shades.
For every shadow, a blessing pervades,
In the soul's path, the heart cascades.

Embrace of the Mysterious Thicket

In the thicket dense, secrets entwine,
Branches whisper, nature's design.
A haven of shadows, soft and divine,
As twilight descends, night's stars align.

The rustle of leaves, a gentle sigh,
An owl calls out from high up in the sky.
A world awakens as darkness draws nigh,
In the thicket's embrace, we learn to fly.

Crickets sing softly, a lullaby sweet,
Where foliage dances, and shadows meet.
Here in the thicket, life's pulses repeat,
The heart finds a rhythm, a blissful heartbeat.

Each moment lingers, time feels unbound,
Lost in the mystery, enchantment profound.
As night drapes its veil over sacred ground,
In this embrace, beauty is found.

With every footfall, a tale unfolds,
Of courage found and dreams retold.
In the thicket's heart, warmth against the cold,
Life's wonders emerge, unbridled and bold.

Flickering Lights Among the Mulfold Leaves

Beneath the boughs where shadows play,
Flickering lights dance in the gray.
Fireflies twinkle, a soft ballet,
Reminders of magic that lingers in sway.

Among the leaves, a hidden glow,
Illuminating paths where whispers flow.
In the gentle night, all worries below,
Forgotten dreams begin to bestow.

Twilight draws close, the world becomes still,
In the hush of dusk, hearts start to fill.
Nature's canvas, a breathtaking thrill,
In flickering lights, a serene goodwill.

Every soft flicker, a promise anew,
Guiding lost souls like morning's dew.
In the canopy's arms, comfort breaks through,
Among the mulfold leaves, hope's vibrant hue.

As the stars awaken, the night sings along,
A melody cherished, a tender song.
In the dance of fireflies, we all belong,
Flickering lights, where spirits grow strong.

Shadowed Tales from the Timeless Grove

In the grove where shadows whisper low,
Tales of the ancients begin to flow.
Each twisted trunk, a story to show,
Of love and loss, of spirits aglow.

The moon casts silver on gnarled branches,
As the heart of the forest quietly dances.
Echoes intertwine, as time enhances,
A melody heard in thought's advances.

Every rustling leaf holds memories dear,
A soft breeze carries laughter and cheer.
In the shadowlands, nothing to fear,
For every sorrow finds solace near.

The timeless grove, where old souls reside,
In the hush of the night, friends bide.
Through shadows and light, they gently guide,
In stories forgotten, wisdom is supplied.

Beneath starlit skies, the heart starts to roam,
In the grove's embrace, we find our home.
With every breath, we weave and comb,
Shadowed tales, our spirits grown.

The Arcane Tapestry of the Wildwood

Threads of green and gold entwined,
Nature's secrets, softly mined.
Winds whisper tales of days gone by,
Beneath the vast and endless sky.

Mossy carpets, shadows cast,
Ancient echoes from the past.
Twilight dances, spirits swirl,
In the heart of the wildwood's pearl.

Charming forms in twilight's glow,
Secrets only few may know.
Branches weave a sacred dance,
Inviting all with a mere glance.

Creatures hidden, eyes agleam,
In the forest's living dream.
Life unfurls in every grove,
A magic here, unseen, but strove.

In wildwood's arms, we find our place,
Woven deep in nature's grace.
The arcane calls, we must reply,
In this tapestry, we fly high.

Frayed Edges of Nature's Mystique

Upon the frayed edges of bliss,
Whispers linger, shadows kiss.
Nature's heart beats soft and low,
In a rhythm only few can know.

Petals scattered, colors blend,
A fading beauty, yet no end.
Threads unravel, life entwined,
In the fabric of the mind.

The river sings a gentle tune,
Underneath the watchful moon.
Time stands still, moments merge,
In the quiet, all souls surge.

Wind-strewn paths, a gentle guide,
Where secrets of the forest hide.
The whispers ebb, the echoes flow,
Nature's mystique, forever glow.

In frayed edges, life starts anew,
A hidden world, a sacred view.
We wander through this fleeting grace,
Finding wonder in each trace.

Moonlit Silhouettes in Whispering Pines

Moonlight drapes the pines so tall,
Casting shadows, beckoning all.
Silhouettes dance in night's embrace,
The forest breathes with quiet grace.

Whispers drift on the cool night air,
Secrets shared, naught left to spare.
Branches sway, a lullaby,
Underneath the starry sky.

Every rustle, every sigh,
Lends a soul to the night sky.
Footsteps soft on ancient ground,
In this realm, pure magic found.

Moonlit paths, an endless maze,
Lost in thought, caught in a daze.
The air is thick with stories old,
In these woods, their truths unfold.

Silhouettes whisper under the moon,
Drawing forth a haunting tune.
In the embrace of nature sweet,
We find our hearts and fears complete.

The Faerie's Lament Among Green Shadows

In shadows deep where faeries play,
A gentle heart begins to sway.
Lost in dreams of ages past,
In emerald glades, their stories last.

Voices soft as summer rain,
Echo through the quiet pain.
A lingering touch of twilight's kiss,
Wraps the world in tender bliss.

Among the leaves, secrets sigh,
Stories woven, wisdom high.
Each lament, a soft refrain,
Filling night with joy and pain.

Glowing orbs of ancient light,
Guide the wanderers of the night.
In the realm where wishes bloom,
Faeries dance, dispelling gloom.

In whispers low, their hearts align,
Carving paths, both dark and fine.
The faerie's lament, a song so true,
Echoes on, forever new.

Lights Flicker in the Whispering Forest

In the hush of twilight's glow,
Where shadows dance and flickers flow.
Stars awaken in the dark,
Guided softly by the spark.

Leaves murmur secrets to the night,
Crickets chirp with sheer delight.
Moonbeams weave through branches old,
Illuminating stories told.

A breeze carries whispers near,
Caught between the trees, so clear.
Each flicker tells of time's embrace,
A fleeting moment, a gentle grace.

Beneath a sky of twinkling dreams,
The forest breathes in softest seams.
Nature's magic beckons low,
Where every light reveals its glow.

As dawn approaches, shadows fade,
Yet in our hearts, the memories stayed.
In every flicker, love remains,
A forever bond in nature's veins.

Fractured Echoes of Timeworn Trees

Ancient bark with lines of lore,
Whispers trapped in knots and more.
Roots entwined beneath the ground,
Fractured echoes all around.

With every breeze, they tell their tale,
Of storms that passed and winds that wail.
Children's laughter, lost in years,
Carried softly along with tears.

Sunlight dapples through the leaves,
Drawing patterns that each tree weaves.
In their silence, wisdom hums,
Tales of ages, time becomes.

Wooden giants hold the past,
Shadows long and memories cast.
In the stillness, listen close,
Hear their echoes, hear them boast.

The forest breathes, it lives, it sighs,
In every crack, a truth belies.
Fractured echoes, yet so strong,
Timeworn trees sing nature's song.

Sorcery Brews in the Verdant Depths

In the heart where ferns entwine,
Sorcery brews with roots divine.
Herbs and blossoms, colors blend,
Magic whispers without end.

Mushrooms dot the forest floor,
Hidden secrets, nature's store.
A potion brews beneath the leaves,
With every sigh, the forest breathes.

Cauldrons bubble, spirits wake,
Elemental forces quake.
In the shadows, a figure stirs,
Casting spells with mystic purrs.

The moonlight dapples on the ground,
In this sanctuary, peace is found.
Omega waves of ancient dreams,
Wrap the forest in silver beams.

From thickets deep to skies so wide,
Nature's magic will abide.
In verdant depths, we trust and see,
The sorcery of wild beauty.

Hidden Tales Beneath the Bark

Underneath the rugged skin,
Lie stories waiting to begin.
Each ring a chapter, year by year,
Whispers of the past so near.

Beetles scurry, life abounds,
In the grove where time resounds.
A universe beneath our feet,
Where tiny worlds and moments meet.

Echoes of the storms endured,
In every crack, the heart secured.
Vines embrace with gentle grace,
Nature's art, a timeless space.

Beneath the bark, the tales are spun,
Of battles lost and victories won.
In silence, wisdom stands apart,
Each notch a piece of nature's heart.

Amongst the roots and shaded glade,
Hidden tales are never swayed.
Time whispers softly through the dark,
Revealing dreams beneath the bark.

The Charms of the Misted Canopy

In whispers low, the branches sway,
A veil of fog, where shadows play.
The sunlight dances, fades away,
Nature's secrets softly stay.

Beneath the leaves, a world concealed,
With tales of life that once revealed.
A gentle breeze, a dream appealed,
In the tranquil morning, healed.

Ferns unfurl in quiet grace,
Each step a breath in this embrace.
The colors blend, a soft lace,
In this enchanted, hidden space.

Mists arise, like spirits roam,
They find solace among the loam.
In this realm, we're not alone,
Together, heartbeats find their home.

Each sigh of wind, a soothing balm,
In nature's arms, we find our calm.
The canopy, a timeless psalm,
Where life's essence stays, a charm.

Melodies of Mutable Trunks

The trunks twist in a thousand ways,
Each knot and curve sings of its days.
From bark to branch, the music plays,
In twilight's warmth, the heart's ablaze.

Rustling leaves, a gentle sound,
In every rustle, magic found.
The woodland stage, with roots renowned,
Nature's hymn, our souls unbound.

Beneath the boughs, the echoes ring,
In harmony, the earth does sing.
A song of life, in every spring,
With every breath, our spirits cling.

The dance of light through shifting trees,
Bringing whispers on the breeze.
They weave a tale with perfect ease,
A symphony that never flees.

In every bend, a story sighs,
The variable trunk beneath the skies.
Within nature's heart, our spirit ties,
As melodies weave 'neath the wide, open skies.

Hidden Reflections in Ebon Boughs

In shadows deep, the secrets gleam,
Reflections dance in a silent stream.
Ebon boughs where the night birds dream,
Whispers of the lost, a mystic theme.

Glimmers shine like stars at dusk,
In the forest's heart, hidden husk.
Every leaf holds a tale, a trust,
In the silence, the unseen must.

Moonlit paths beneath the dark,
Illuminated with a spark.
Each tree a sentinel, leaves embark,
Guiding souls through dusk till hark.

The pensive air, with stories spun,
In every rustle, a tale begun.
Life unfolds where shadows run,
Reflections glow; the journey's fun.

Within the depths of twilight's hold,
Nature's beauty starts to unfold.
In every branch, a mystery told,
A realm alive, both young and old.

Heartbeats Among the Enchanted Glade

In the glade where dreams collide,
Heartbeat rhythms soft and wide.
In nature's arms, we quiet abide,
Among the whispers, side by side.

Sunlight dapples through the leaves,
Nature breathes, and the spirit heaves.
In this place, the heart believes,
In magic moments, love conceives.

Wildflowers bloom, a vibrant show,
Their colors dance, a gentle flow.
In this haven, smiles readily grow,
Among the glade, where soft winds blow.

The murmurs of the brook nearby,
Carry tales of the earth and sky.
In every drop, our hopes can fly,
A peaceful space where none comply.

As twilight falls, the stars ignite,
In the glade, the world feels right.
Together wrapped in this delight,
Our heartbeats pulse, a shared insight.

Dance of the Arcane Saplings

In moonlit glades where shadows play,
Young saplings dance at end of day.
Their whispers float on gentle breeze,
Pendulums swaying among the trees.

Mystic lights flicker, warm and bright,
Guiding the way through tranquil night.
Each rooted spirit sways with grace,
A hidden world in a sacred space.

With every rustle, secrets told,
Of ancient magic, bright and bold.
The air alive with tales untold,
Of starlit paths and leaves of gold.

Through tangled twigs and emerald hue,
Genre of dreams, to hearts be true.
Whirling wonders, a timeless dance,
Allured by fate and moonbeam's trance.

As dawn unfolds with golden light,
Saplings stir from dreams of night.
With hope renewed, they seek to rise,
And greet the sun, 'neath widening skies.

Nature's Veil of Spellbound Leaves

Underneath a leafy dome,
Nature weaves a world of home.
Every leaf a tale does weave,
Whispers soft, we pause and grieve.

A tapestry of colors spun,
Brushing skies with warmth of sun.
Crimson hues and golds ablaze,
In nature's grasp, we surely gaze.

Amidst the trees, enchantments flow,
Secret paths where few may go.
Brushing fingers on emerald beds,
Gentle sighs of nature spreads.

Beneath the boughs, the fae do play,
In sunlight's glow, they laugh and sway.
They twirl and weave, a mystic flight,
In nature's veil, pure delight.

As twilight wraps the world in dreams,
Hopeful echoes, silent screams.
The leaves shiver, a gentle night,
Nature's charm, a soft respite.

Tendrils of the Forgotten Realm

In shadows deep, the tendrils creep,
Luring souls from dreams of sleep.
Through haunted woods and rugged stone,
Lives a magic all its own.

Veils of mist like whispered sighs,
Hide the stars in velvet skies.
Ancient roots with secrets bind,
Echoes lost for hearts to find.

Tendrils brave, seeking the light,
Woven paths through endless night.
Echoing tales of ages past,
A forgotten lore, forever vast.

Each twist and turn, a tale unfurls,
Of phantom realms and shimmering pearls.
Guided by the moon's embrace,
Dancing dreams in ethereal grace.

Fingers brush against the past,
In gentle whispers, spells are cast.
A hidden world where shadows loom,
Tendrils weave their mystic bloom.

Roots Entwined in Arcane Lore

In the soil where shadows grow,
Roots entwined, a tale we sow.
Whispers ancient, soft and pure,
Nature's magic, strong and sure.

Bound in earth, secrets lie,
In the depths, where spirits sigh.
The dance of roots leads to the night,
In arcs of wonder, taking flight.

From craggy rock to fertile seam,
They weave a web of ancient dream.
Brushing against each dusky stone,
Entwined in magic, never alone.

Each tendril speaks of love and loss,
In echoes of the forest's gloss.
With whispered vows beneath the ground,
In this realm, true peace is found.

As morning dew adorns the leaves,
We feel the magic that nature weaves.
With every breath, we sow the lore,
Embraced by roots forevermore.

Starlit Trails Beneath the Canopy

Beneath the stars, where shadows play,
The whispering leaves sway night away.
Moonlight dances on the forest floor,
Guiding dreams to an endless shore.

Crickets sing a soft lullaby,
As fireflies flicker, painting the sky.
Each step echoes through ancient trees,
Carried softly by the night breeze.

A tapestry woven from silver light,
Starlit trails lead on in the night.
Nature's secrets gently unfold,
In the warmth of stories retold.

The world in stillness, hearts entwined,
In this sacred space, we find peace of mind.
Breathless moments, forever they linger,
As magic whispers, beckoning fingers.

A symphony of wonders, vast and deep,
In starlit trails, our souls forever leap.
Through nature's arms, we find our way,
Beneath this canopy, forever stay.

The Dance of Enchanted Twill

In twilight's glow, the fabric sways,
Threads of wonder in soft array.
Patterns swirling in the evening air,
Whispers of secrets, a dance so rare.

Spinning tales of moonlit grace,
Each twill a heartbeat in this place.
Colors shimmer, intertwine,
In the fabric of dreams, so divine.

A gentle rhythm, a soft refrain,
As stars above watch the dance sustain.
An embrace of night, a lover's call,
Wrapped in enchantment, we lose it all.

Embroidered whispers of ages past,
Every stitch a story, forever to last.
In the realm of dreams, we find our role,
Bound by the threads that connect the soul.

The dance of twill, both bold and meek,
In every fold, the heart can speak.
Through twinkling eyes, we spin and twirl,
In this enchanted fabric, we unfurl.

Spirits of the Sylvan Domain

Whispers echo through ancient wood,
Spirits dwell where nature stood.
Elusive shadows dance in play,
Guardians of night and breaking day.

Mossy trunks and emerald ferns,
In their presence, the heart returns.
A flicker of hope in twilight's embrace,
The sylvan spirits watch our pace.

Beneath the boughs of time-worn trees,
Life unfurls with graceful ease.
In harmony with every sigh,
The sylvan souls linger nearby.

Echoes of laughter, stories retold,
In every rustle, their spirits bold.
Step lightly where the wild things roam,
In this domain, we find our home.

Their wisdom flows like rivers wide,
In every heartbeat, they abide.
Embrace their warmth, let the stillness reign,
In the sylvan realm, we find our gain.

Luminescence Wrapped in Nature's Embrace

Amidst the trees, a gentle glow,
Nature's touch begins to show.
Wrapped in hues of amber light,
A secret world awakens from night.

Softly shining through leaves above,
Whispers of magic, a tale of love.
Every petal draped in gleaming fire,
Nature's canvas, an artist's desire.

In the heart of dusk, the luminescence blooms,
Painting shadows, dissolving glooms.
A symphony of light, a radiant sea,
Where every creature moves wild and free.

With every step, the magic we trace,
In nature's embrace, we find our place.
Illumined paths, guiding the way,
Through the embrace of the end of day.

Together we walk in this shimmering dream,
Under the stars, the world will beam.
Wrapped in wonder, our spirits will soar,
In nature's embrace, forevermore.

Serenade of the Wandering Roots

Beneath the canopy so wide,
The roots entwine with quiet pride.
Whispers of earth in twilight's hum,
Their dance begins as shadows come.

From ancient wells they seek to find,
The tales of years, both lost and blind.
Each gnarled twist a story spun,
Of paths once walked, now overrun.

With jagged dreams and silent sighs,
They stretch towards the endless skies.
In every crack, a secret waits,
Entwined in fate, as time abates.

A serenade of whispers calls,
Through winding trails and ancient halls.
The roots, they mingle, twist, and sway,
In search of hope along the way.

As night descends, the world does sleep,
The wandering roots in silence keep.
Yet in their depths, a fire glows,
Of life reclaimed where wildness flows.

Fading Dreams Under the Leafy Arc

Beneath the leaves, where shadows play,
The dreams of youth begin to sway.
In gentle whispers, soft and low,
Fading echoes of long-lost glow.

The arc of green, a fleeting view,
Holds secrets of the old and new.
A tapestry of dusk and dawn,
In every rustle, a breath drawn.

Twilight casts a fleeting spell,
Where haunted tales begin to swell.
Each moment drifts like falling dew,
Embracing dreams that fade from view.

Yet in the stillness, hope will rise,
Like whispered truths beneath the skies.
Through leaves that dance, a heart will mend,
And dreams once lost will find their blend.

In this embrace of night and day,
The leafy arc shall guide the way.
For even as the shadows creep,
A promise stirs, in silence deep.

Nature's Palette in Twilight's Glow

In twilight's glow, hues intertwine,
Nature's brush paints lines divine.
With every stroke, a story blooms,
In vibrant shades that banish gloom.

The sky a canvas, vast and clear,
Soft whispers of the night draw near.
Gold and crimson, a fleeting show,
A dance of colors, ebb and flow.

The trees stand tall, silhouettes bold,
Guardians of the dreams retold.
Each leaf a whisper, sweet refrain,
In the dusk's heart, life finds its gain.

As stars awaken, softly bright,
They join the dance, a wondrous sight.
Together they weave the cosmic thread,
In twilight's glow, all worries shed.

Nature's palette sings so sweet,
With rhythm of hearts, where spirits meet.
Embracing the night, the wild, the free,
In colors bright, we find our glee.

Fragments of Time in Twisted Wood

In twisted wood, where shadows linger,
Fragments of time grasp at each finger.
The knots and bends of bark tell tales,
Of storms endured, and whispered gales.

Each carved groove, a memory holds,
Of dreams once bright and actions bold.
The echoes of footsteps, soft and faint,
In every twist, a ghostly paint.

Beneath the canopy, secrets unfold,
Nature writes stories in hues of gold.
As seasons pass, a gentle sigh,
In twisted wood, where spirits fly.

Branches intertwine, a woven screen,
Of past and present, rarely seen.
The laughter of leaves, in soft embrace,
Reminds the heart of its rightful place.

So let us wander through this maze,
In search of truth, in nature's gaze.
For in each fragment, life renews,
In twisted wood, our souls imbue.

Legendary Echoes in Living Veins

Whispers of giants long gone,
Flow through the heart of the earth.
Their tales dance in the shadows,
Awakening spirits of worth.

Mountains stand tall, bearing truth,
Ancient echoes in every stone.
In valleys where dreams dare to breathe,
Legends are never alone.

Rivers run wild with memories,
Each current a song from the past.
Legends entwined in living veins,
A bond that forever will last.

Through the forests, secrets hum,
In the rustle of each worn leaf.
Nature sings of heroic deeds,
And gives both solace and grief.

Time flows like a river unbound,
Stories surfacing, deep and clear.
In living veins, legends arise,
Forever echoing near.

The Dreams Carved in Knotted Grasp

In twisted roots of time we find,
Dreams carved deep in knotted grasp.
Whispers of wishes long obscured,
Awakening in shadows, clasp.

Branches weave a tapestry,
Of hopes that linger in the night.
Fragrant blossoms soft and rare,
Echoing their muted light.

Underneath a moonlit veil,
Gentle thoughts begin to sway.
In silence, visions bloom anew,
Guided by the stars' ballet.

The night reveals its secret paths,
Where dreams and destinies entwine.
Each knot a tale, each twist a choice,
In the grasp of dreams divine.

With every dawn, the promise grows,
Of journeys yet to be unlocked.
In knotted grasp, we find our way,
On paths that fate has chalked.

Celestial Canopy and the Hidden Lore

Under a dome of sparkling sighs,
Stars weave tales of old and bright.
Celestial lore in silence shared,
Illuminates the deep of night.

Each constellation holds a key,
To secrets whispered by the breeze.
In cosmic dance, the stories twirl,
As time bends gently with such ease.

Ancient eyes watch from above,
Guardians of dreams we hold dear.
They guide the lost with gentle light,
Filling shadows with hope and cheer.

Beneath this canopy of grace,
Hidden lore awakens the heart.
In every twinkle, wisdom beams,
Filling each void with a spark.

The universe sings to those who hear,
In cosmic rhythm, tales unfold.
Celestial canopies embrace,
And cradle legends untold.

Tangles of Magic Beneath the Stars

In the web of night, magic weaves,
Tangles of dreams, bright and rare.
Beneath the stars, enchantment swirls,
Floating lightly in the air.

Glowing orbs of endless grace,
Dance in harmony above.
They whisper secrets, soft and low,
Of hidden worlds and lost love.

Each flicker tells a story true,
Of long-lost paths and fates entwined.
In the silence of the dark,
Magic's tender threads aligned.

Beneath the vast celestial dome,
Wonders stir in tender embrace.
With every heartbeat, stories grow,
In this enchanted, sacred space.

Beneath the stars, we find our dreams,
Wrapped in tangles, wild and free.
Magic blooms where hearts collide,
Igniting wild destinies.

Tapestry Woven in Green Chaos

Leaves dance in the sunlight's gaze,
Threads of nature's vibrant maze.
Breezes twirl in gentle delight,
Life unfurls in emerald light.

Branches weave a tale untold,
Secrets in the rustling fold.
Whispers echo, a mystical sound,
In this haven, peace is found.

Amidst the clamor of chaotic song,
Every heartbeat feels so strong.
Nature's quilt, a blend so rare,
In this chaos, love and care.

Colors merge, a painter's dream,
In the chaos, joy does gleam.
An artist strokes with deft embrace,
Crafting peace in nature's space.

Tapestry of life, rich and bright,
In the heart of the forest's light.
Woven threads both loose and tight,
In green chaos, a pure delight.

The Lullaby of Forest's Heart

In the shadows, soft and deep,
Nature hums the world to sleep.
Crickets play a soothing tune,
Underneath the watchful moon.

Rustling leaves in sweet embrace,
Cradle dreams in nature's grace.
The gentle night calls out to me,
In this realm, I'm truly free.

Mighty oaks lend strength and peace,
In their arms, my worries cease.
A symphony of silent sighs,
Softly lingers, as time flies.

Stars twinkle above with care,
Illuminating the night air.
Each breath in this tranquil space,
Reminds me of love's warm face.

Hush now, world, let dreams take flight,
In the forest's heart tonight.
Wrapped in twilight, calm and smart,
I find solace, a work of art.

Swaying Whispers of the Elder Boughs

Gnarled branches reach for the sky,
Whispers of the ages sigh.
Time has gifted them with grace,
Stories linger, secrets trace.

Leaves flutter with a knowing sound,
Echoes of the past abound.
In the breeze, they share their lore,
Of ancient roots and life before.

Swaying gently, they create a song,
A melody where hearts belong.
Guiding spirits through twilight's glow,
In their presence, wisdom flows.

Beneath the boughs, I sit and dream,
Lost in nature's flowing stream.
The world dissolves, as I embrace,
The sacred space, a tranquil place.

Elder whispers brush my skin,
Inviting me to dwell within.
In this dance, the heart's profound,
In swaying whispers, love is found.

Mirage of Sylvan Shadows

In a glen where shadows play,
Dreams unfold and drift away.
Mirages dance beneath the trees,
Swaying lightly in the breeze.

Calls of creatures, soft and clear,
Invite the wanderer near.
Nature holds a sacred space,
Where time slows, and fears embrace.

Fern and moss create the floor,
Invite me in to seek and explore.
Through the mist, a figure glides,
In the twilight where magic resides.

Ethereal light guides my way,
As the shadows softly sway.
In this realm of hushed delight,
I find solace in the night.

Mirage of beauty, hope, and grace,
In the sylvan shadows, I find my place.
Embraced by nature, wild and free,
In this dream, I am meant to be.

www.ingramcontent.com/pod-product-compliance
Ingram Content Group UK Ltd.
Pitfield, Milton Keynes, MK11 3LW, UK
UKHW021535210125
4208UKWH00025B/646